AN AQUARIAN EXPOSITION:

3 DAYS OF PEACE & MUSIC

August 15, 16, and 17, 1969. Woodstock Music & Art Fair organizers expected 50,000 attendees. They'd had trouble securing a venue until dairy farmer Max Yasgur agreed to let them use his 600-acre farm in Bethel, New York. Until April, they'd also had trouble signing popular performers. But when the festival began, more than 400,000 attendees arrived. By the time it ended, 32 of the most iconic rock and folk acts of the 1960s had taken the stage. They played in the sun, the rain, and the middle of the night. Rock & roll legends were created, a generation was defined, and music was changed forever.

FRIDAY

5:07	Richie Havens
7:10	invocation from Swami Satchidananda
7:30	Sweetwater
8:20	Bert Sommer
9:20	Tim Hardin
10:00	Ravi Shankar
10:50	Melanie
11:55	Arlo Guthrie
12:55	Joan Baez

SATURDAY

12:15	Quill
1:00	Country Joe McDonald
2:00	Santana
3:30	John Sebastian
4:45	Keef Hartley Band
6:00	The Incredible String Band
7:30	Canned Heat
9:00	Mountain
10:30	Grateful Dead
12:30	Creedence Clearwater Revival
2:00	Janis Joplin with the Kozmic Blues Band
3:30	Sly and the Family Stone
5:00	The Who
8:00	Jefferson Airplane

SUNDAY

2:00	Joe Cocker and the Grease Band
6:30	Country Joe and the Fish
8:15	Ten Years After
10:00	The Band
12:00	Johnny Winter
1:30	Blood, Sweat & Tears
3:00	Crosby, Stills, Nash & Young
6:00	Paul Butterfield Blues Band
7:30	Sha Na Na
9:00	Jimi Hendrix/Gypsy Sun & Rainbows

WELCOME TO YOUR DOT JOURNAL.

Here is your chance to organize, develop new habits, track your goals, make notes, and stimulate your creativity. Find a pen (or set of pens) you love, carry your journal with you, and get planning!

MAKE A KEY.

You'll be making a lot of lists in your dot journal—things to do, observations, steps toward a goal, and more. Use the first page of your journal as a key to the symbols you'll use to note them. Perhaps a to-do list item that requires action is preceded by a dot or a checkbox. When you finish the item, change the dot to an X or make a check in the box. If you move it to the next day's to-do list, change the dot to an arrow. Keep track of your symbols on the key, and feel free to add more or change them once you get a feel for how you're actually using your journal.

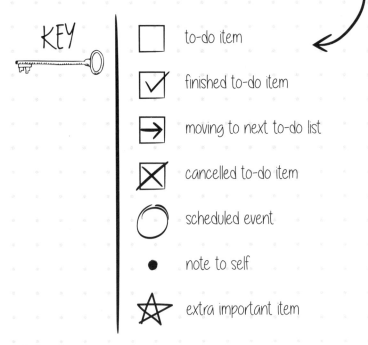

KEY

- ☐ to-do item
- ☑ finished to-do item
- → moving to next to-do list
- ☒ cancelled to-do item
- ◯ scheduled event
- ● note to self
- ☆ extra important item

INDEX IT.

Reserve the next few pages of your journal to index the pages as you go. You'll be setting schedules, managing to-do lists, tracking your goals, and more all over this journal, and a handy table of contents will help you find the page you need quickly. When you start a new page, record its title and page number in your index. Whenever you make notes about a certain topic—a goal, planning a trip, etc.—add the page number to the index.

INDEX

MAKE A CALENDAR.

Use your dot journal as a planner. Start with a big-picture view, use a spread or two to draw or outline a calendar of the year, the school year, or whatever length of time you find helpful. Give each month a section. When someone says, "Want to come to my concert in May?" even though it is still February, just jot down the date in the May section. No more stress about potentially missing concerts!

2018

JANUARY
6th Erica's dinner party, 6pm
8th Q&L presentation, 11am
14th Pepper to vet, 2pm

FEBRUARY
Schedule car maintenance
Email Michelle @ Pres

MARCH
8th dentist

APRIL

MAY

JUNE
16th Sarah & Mo's wedding

JULY

AUGUST

SEPTEMBER

OCTOBER

NOVEMBER

DECEMBER

You might also want to add monthly and weekly calendar spreads as they begin or you start to plan them in earnest. These pages can be as simple or complicated as you'd like. Write the month at the top of the page, draw a line or a box for each day of the month, and start transferring in appointments from your big-picture calendar.

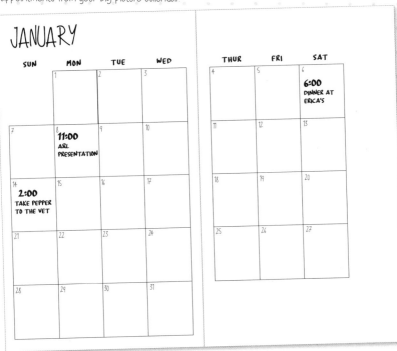

Keep your daily lists nearby or on these pages, too. Add everything: your to-do action items, notes about your day, appointments you need to attend, stray thoughts, etc. Use a symbol from your key to begin each line.

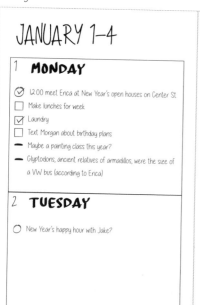

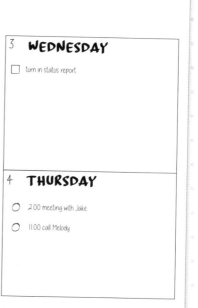

SET GOALS.

Few things you can do are as beneficial as setting and tracking goals. They help you focus and get stuff done, of course, but they also help motivate you and give you a sense of purpose and accomplishment—ultimately making you a happier, more effective person. So use this journal to set some goals!

First, set aside some uninterrupted time to really think about your dreams. Write them down. When you're satisfied with the list (for now), start setting goals that will help you reach those dreams. Make the goals as specific and easily measurable as you can. That is, instead of "read more," make your goal "read 52 books this year" or "read for an average of 1 hour every day." Your goals should be challenging but doable. If they're too hard, you'll give up; if they're too easy, there's no point.

You could try setting goals, for example, for your personal development, your creative life, your family life, your relationship, your health, your career, and/or your finances. The possibilities are as limitless as your dreams. Go to town!

Here's where your dot journal really shines: it's time to choose a goal and break it down into steps. Turn to a blank page in your journal and think of the best way to visualize your goal. For example, let's say your goal is "Read 52 books this year." You could simply write your goal at the top of the page, and number it from 1 to 52. When you finish a book, you'll turn to this page and add the title to the next numbered line. Or, maybe you know you'll respond well to checkboxes—if so, start making empty squares. Got an artistic streak? Maybe you'll draw shelves containing 52 books and write the titles on the spines as you finish them. Want to add another timing element? Organize it by month. This could mean drawing a calendar, or it could mean changing the color of the numbers every four or five lines. The important part is finding a method that appeals to you.

Now comes the hard part. Get started. Work on your goal, track it in your journal, and get right back to it. When you screw up (when, not if), that's okay. Look how far you've come, forgive yourself, and keep going. And when you reach your goal? Celebrate!

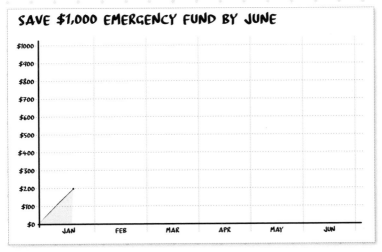

SAVE $1,000 EMERGENCY FUND BY JUNE

READ 52 BOOKS THIS YEAR.

1. Ready Player One
2. All Your Worth
3. The Great Gatsby
4. Spark Joy
5.
6.
7.
8.
9.
10.
11.
12.
13.
14.
15.
16.
17.
18.
19.
20.
21.
22.
23.
24.
25.
26.

27.
28.
29.
30.
31.
32.
33.
34.
35.
36.
37.
38.
39.
40.
41.
42.
43.
44.
45.
46.
47.
48.
49.
50.
51.
52.

MAKE NOTES.

This journal is meant to accompany you through the day, so it's more than an elaborate to-do list. It's also a record of your life and an opportunity to explore your creativity. Try adding notes about what happens or quotes you want to remember to your daily list, using a different symbol to set them off. Try freewriting on a new page to expand on those ideas, if you'd like. Sketch your surroundings. Doodle in the margins. Do whatever works for you in order to organize your life, reach your goals, and engage your creativity.

Get started!

ISBN 978-1-64178-016-2

COPY PERMISSION: The written instructions, photographs, designs, patterns, and projects in this publication are intended for the personal use of the reader and may be reproduced for that purpose only. Any other use, especially commercial use, is forbidden under law without the written permission of the copyright holder.
NOTE: The use of products and trademark names is for informational purposes only, with no intention of infringement upon those trademarks.

Fox Chapel Publishing makes every effort to use environmentally friendly paper for printing.

We are always looking for talented authors. To submit an idea, please send a brief inquiry to acquisitions@foxchapelpublishing.com.

© 2018 Woodstock Ventures, LC. Under License to Epic Rights/Perryscope Productions LLC and Quiet Fox Designs, an imprint of Fox Chapel Publishing, 800-457-9112, 903 Square Street, Mount Joy, PA 17552.

Printed in China
First printing

13

27

29

46

55